IMAGES
of America

DODDRIDGE AND RITCHIE COUNTIES

Robert F. Stealey

ISBN 978-1-5316-0931-3

Published by Arcadia Publishing,
Charleston, South Carolina

Library of Congress Catalog Card Number: 2001090008

For all general information contact Arcadia Publishing at:
Telephone 843-853-2070
Fax 843-853-0044
E-Mail sales@arcadiapublishing.com
For customer service and orders:
Toll-Free 1-888-313-2665

Visit us on the Internet at www.arcadiapublishing.com

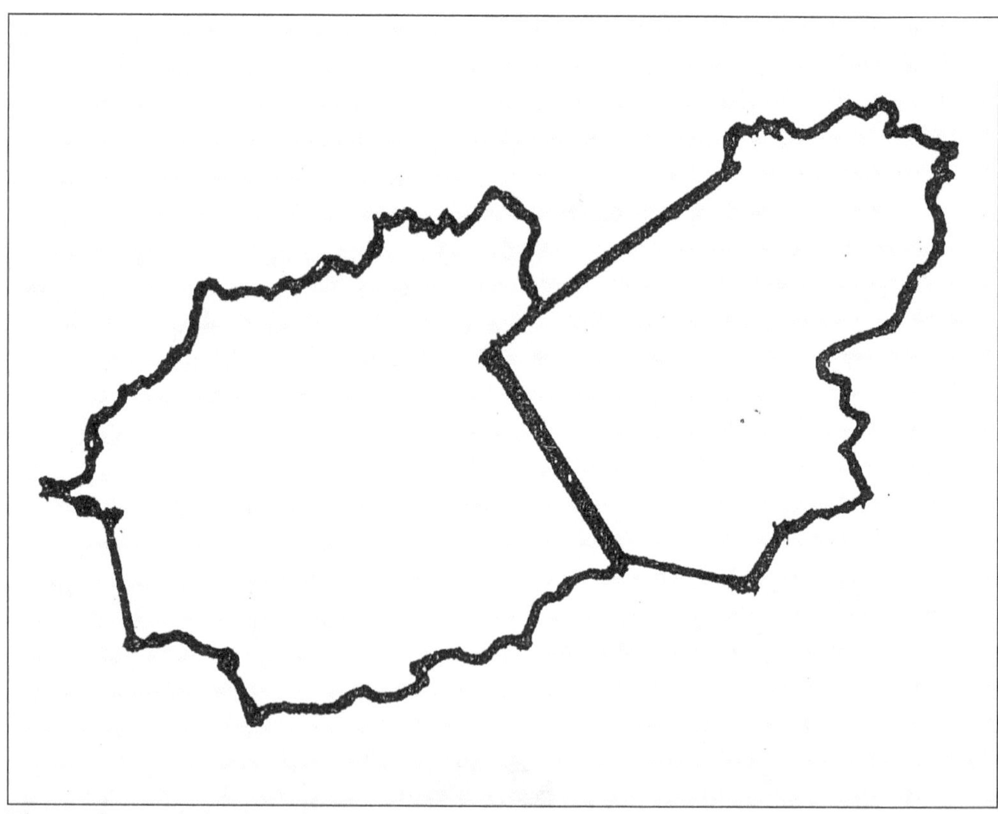

The outlines of the boundaries of Doddridge and Ritchie Counties are pictured above. Doddridge, at right, is the more eastern county, although smaller in area than Ritchie.

Contents

ACKNOWLEDGMENTS

Images of America: Doddridge and Ritchie Counties might never have been possible if it were not for the generous provision of photographs and images from Bill Calhoun, president of the Doddridge County Historical Society, and David Scott, president of the Ritchie County Historical Society. Photos from several binders kept for exhibit in the museum of the Doddridge County Historical Society have proven invaluable. Also, a number of original images from *A Photographic History of Ritchie County, West Virginia* by the Ritchie County Historical Society, published in 1989 by Walsworth Publishing Co. of Marceline, Missouri—now out of print—have been used in this work.

I would like to also thank Larry G. Williams Sr. of Munroe Falls, Ohio, for making available a number of other original photos that appear in both the Doddridge County and Ritchie County divisions of my book.

Some data was also derived from *The History of Doddridge County, West Virginia*, copyrighted in 1979 by the Doddridge County Historical Society and printed by Taylor Publishing Co. of Dallas, Texas, and Paoli, Pennsylvania.

In addition, I would like to thank my wife, Nadine L. Stealey, for her support during the weeks that I spent my evenings preparing this work, and also for the patience and guidance of my editor, Laura E. Daniels, and previous editor, Christine T. Riley.

Introduction

The counties of Doddridge and Ritchie in northern West Virginia have quite a number of similarities, although they are different in geographic area. Both have a common history of rich resources of oil and gas, railroads, and timber from the 19th and early 20th centuries.

Located just west of Harrison County, Doddridge was organized in 1845 from portions of Tyler, Lewis, Harrison, and Ritchie Counties. It was named in honor of Phillip Doddridge, an eminent Virginian and statesman (1750–1832), the same year it was organized. The land on which the town of West Union, the seat of Doddridge County, stands was patented c. 1787 by James Caldwell. It is located on the south bank of Middle Island Creek, widely believed to be the longest creek in the nation. For years, West Union was a supply point for a vast oil territory, with productive oil fields to the north and the south.

Just east of Wood County, Ritchie County was formed in 1843 from portions of the counties of Harrison, Lewis, and Wood. It was named for Thomas Ritchie, a distinguished journalist from Richmond, Virginia, whose mother was the sister of Judge Spencer Roane, for whom the adjacent Roane County was named. Ritchie County's seat of Harrisville was laid out in 1822 on land in the wilderness that was owned by Thomas Harris. Its first post office was established 11 years later. The first store in Ritchie County was opened in Harrisville in the early 19th century, and the town was incorporated on February 26, 1869.

While the Baltimore & Ohio Railroad and various other railroad lines provided the main links between Doddridge and Ritchie Counties in previous times, today the primary artery through each is a modern, highly accessible, four-lane highway—U.S. Route 50, which was one of the first roads in the Appalachian Regional Commission's Appalachian Development Corridor Highway System to be completed in the 1970s. Old Route 50 had been a narrow, hilly, winding road, separating Clarksburg and Parkersburg by 81 miles, or more than two hours of driving time. When all links of U.S. Highway 50 were opened, residents of West Union found that they were now only about 25 miles west of Clarksburg. Similarly, Highway 50 places residents of towns like Pennsboro, Ellenboro, Harrisville, and Cairo within 30 minutes of Parkersburg, located on the Ohio River. If the lumbering and oil and gas well industries of the past could have used today's Route 50 for transporting goods, who knows what business opportunities might have evolved?

Wherever one may go in either of the counties of Doddridge or Ritchie, he or she will discover that the residents of each are quite proud of their communities and of their heritage.

Part I

DODDRIDGE COUNTY

Named in honor of Phillip Doddridge, an able lawyer and statesman, Doddridge County is located in the north central region of West Virginia where the elevation seldom reaches a height of 300 feet above the surrounding valleys. Created through a division of Harrison, Ritchie, Tyler, and Lewis Counties, the county consists of 321.61 square miles and is divided into eight magisterial districts, including Central, Grant, Cove, New Milton, Greenbrier, South West, McClellan, and West Union. Well-watered, the county is drained primarily by Middle Island Creek and its tributaries.

At one time, Doddridge County was a wilderness in which no white man had lived and Native American tribes had roamed at will. The earliest record of habitation in the county is an account of a man named James Caldwell who acquired the title to 20,000 acres of land in Doddridge County and sold it to Nathan, Joseph, and William Davis around 1807.

One

Past Generations

The following images of rural folk in the Doddridge County of several generations ago are intended to show the close-knit spirit of these fine people, a great many whom overcame formidable obstacles presented by the terrain of the area and the lack of modern-day conveniences. These citizens enjoyed being photographed in groups and shared in a common desire to see their communities prosper. This chapter reflects the pride that Doddridge County folks have kept alive over the years.

Ovid and Letha Watson are shown here, c. 1944, with their four children. From left to right are Paul, Adalea, Yonna (Nonnie), and Jean. This photo was taken along River Road, off Oxford Road in southwestern Doddridge County. Ovid and Letha later had at least two more children. (Courtesy Larry Williams Sr.)

The home of Mr. and Mrs. David Hinzman and his family near West Union is shown here. The Hinzmans are seated while their son John (left) and daughter Stata Hinzman Thompson (right) stand behind them. Allie Hinzman Lawson, another daughter of the Hinzmans, took this photograph. (Courtesy Doddridge County Historical Society.)

This cameo photograph shows the clerks, or "The Four Orphans," at the Racket Store in New Milton. The title of the photo display, donated by Hazel Douglas, is "Love of Ages." (Courtesy Doddridge County Historical Society.)

The "new" Doddridge County Courthouse is shown above upon its completion in 1904. Jacob Cupp and Jim Davisson may be included in this photo, as they were awarded the contract for completing the basement. Others in the image, donated by Alton Childers, are unidentified. (Courtesy Doddridge County Historical Society.)

These people enjoy an open-air bus ride along a West Union street in the early 20th century. (Courtesy Doddridge County Historical Society.)

Unfortunately, no identifications were available for the individuals shown here, but they all appear to be members of a late 19th- or early 20th-century organization. Can you identify any of the men in this photograph donated by the Oma Corder Estate? (Courtesy Doddridge County Historical Society.)

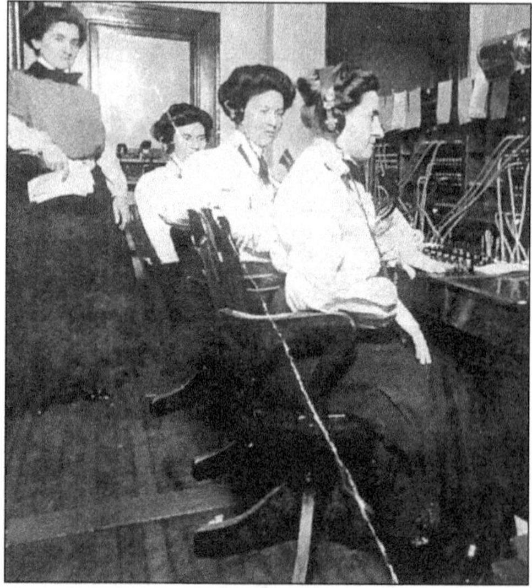

(Left) Taken in August 1939 in West Union, this picture, donated by Jo and Art Dotson, shows Myron E. Smith of Pittsburgh, Pennsylvania (left), Charles J. Hardesty (center), and Laman Leavine. (Courtesy Doddridge County Historical Society.)
(Right) Taken from a postcard, this image, donated by the John and Hattie Hafer Estate, shows a group of telephone operators in Doddridge County. Their supervisor observes them from the background. (Courtesy Doddridge County Historical Society.)

Alton Childers, a Doddridge County historian who wrote numerous articles for the *West Union Herald* newspaper, owned this print, but very little is known about the content of the image. (Courtesy Doddridge County Historical Society.)

(Left) From left to right are Franklin Myers, Howard Myers (on his horse named "Fan"), and Adam Smith. Nellie Smith Swentzel donated this photograph. (Courtesy Doddridge County Historical Society.)
(Right) Pictured here is Adam Smith, this time with his step-grandson Howard Myers, as they hoe corn in Doddridge County. (Courtesy Doddridge County Historical Society.)

At left is the wedding photo of Harry Maxwell and Lettie Davis Maxwell, which was donated by Elsa Maxwell Garrison Lynch. (Courtesy Doddridge County Historical Society.)

Shown here is a churn that was invented by A.H. Stutler in the late 19th century. He never patented it due to some controversy that existed, although he made several. A.H. Stutler was the father of Cecil Stutler, who donated the photo. (Courtesy Doddridge County Historical Society.)

This *c.* 1914 picture was taken on Nancy Swisher Harris's 100th birthday. Swisher is seen in the middle of the first row, holding a small child. Her father, Jacob Swisher, enlisted in the military in 1775 from Berks County, Pennsylvania, and fought in the Revolutionary War. Mrs. Harris's great-great-great granddaughter is Linda Strickling of Route 2, West Union. Included in this group are Trenna Harris, John Harris, Emma Harris, Gertie Harris, Ellen Harris, Buster Harris, Eleazer Freeman, Flora Martin, Mary Freeman, Lemar Underwood, Oliver Orr, Mrs. Harris's grandson Charlie Harris, Flora Harris, Dollie Harris, Anthony Harris, Sarah Duckworth, Walter Duckworth, George B. Orr, and Henry Duckworth. (Courtesy Linda Strickling.)

Judge M.H. Willis, pictured here in the late 1800s, was born in 1862 at Mole Hill, now Mountain, in Ritchie County. He began his career as a teacher, later becoming senior member of the Willis & Stuck law firm in West Union. The Ireland Estate donated the photo. (Courtesy Doddridge County Historical Society.)

Jackson V. Blair, a Harrison County native, was born in 1853 and was a stockholder in and attorney for the West Union Bank. He declined a nomination for judge of the Fourth Judicial Circuit at the Middlebourne Convention in 1896. Jackie Wetzel and the Ireland Estate donated this photo. (Courtesy Doddridge County Historical Society.)

This photo was taken at the E. Nicholas Orr and Ann Johnston Orr reunion that was held August 15, 1914, on Barnes Run near Wallace, at the home of E.D. Orr. From left to right are (first row) Oliver Orr, Margaret S. Orr Freeman, George Freeman, Harriett Ann Orr Underwood, and Hiram Underwood; (second row) George Kester, Victoria Orr Kester, Amanda Nichols, Ida Smith, Costello Underwood, and George V. Nichols; (third row) Harry Underwood, William Orr, Alvy Underwood, Leonias Underwood, and George B. Underwood. (Courtesy Linda Strickling.)

Seated, from left to right, are Rhulana and Adam (Schmidt) Smith with their family behind them. This image was donated by Nettie Smith Swentzel. (Courtesy Doddridge County Historical Society.)

Here, a Doddridge County man sits at a small table with an old-fashioned cylinder record player. Burdett and Barbara Warder donated the photo. (Courtesy Doddridge County Historical Society.)

Hall Maxwell, clerk of the Doddridge County Court for more than 50 years ago, is shown at his courthouse desk. He died July 17, 1955. (Courtesy Doddridge County Historical Society.)

Mrs. Stella Twyford and her children, Delphia and Mayme, appear in the photograph at right. (Courtesy Doddridge County Historical Society.)

Members of the Department of Public Assistance appear in the Doddridge County Courthouse in the 1938 photo below, donated by Jacqueline Wetzel. Alice Pease is at the typewriter. Others said to be in the photo include Mary Ireland, Robert Grey, Rella Hickman, Hazel Fisher, George Bland, and Lana Digman. (Courtesy Doddridge County Historical Society.)

These individuals are shown breaking ground for the Reorganized Church of Jesus Christ of Latter Day Saints near West Union some time in the 1950s, according to Larry G. Williams Sr. of Munroe Falls, Ohio, who provided the photo. The former West Virginian said the church was located at the bottom of Jaco Hill, west of West Union. He identified the trio to be, from left to right, Brother ? Rice, Betty Emerson, and Florence Calhoun Williams, who was his grandmother and an aunt of Bill Calhoun, the president of the Doddridge County Historical Society.

Larry G. Williams is seen as a youngster with his mother, Lucy McIntyre Williams, standing in front of a 1937 knee-action, floor-shift Chevrolet along old U.S. Route 50 at the "Smithburg Cut." The photo was probably taken in 1942 or 1943.

Isaiah Hurtig and Abe Goodman of Hot Springs, Arkansas, appear in this January 10, 1910 image accompanied by a bull with mule feet, considered quite unique. The Ireland Estate donated this photo. (Courtesy Doddridge County Historical Society.)

Gale Knight of the West Virginia State Police at West Union takes a call at his desk in this 1940s photo donated by Betty J. Langfitt. (Courtesy Doddridge County Historical Society.)

Cecil Stutler and "Doc" Platt are the two men riding this horse-drawn buggy. The old Masonic Hall in West Union can be seen in the background of this photo, donated by the Stutler Estate. (Courtesy Doddridge County Historical Society.)

These Doddridge County officials stand outside the courthouse in the mid-20th century. In the photo, donated by Earl Davis, are L.W. Chapman, prosecuting attorney; Floyd Boner, Okey Gallion, and Alva Ash of the county court; Porter Summers, deputy sheriff; V.G. Stinespring, field deputy; Dick Tucker, sheriff; Earl L. Davis, circuit clerk; A.C. Stutler, assessor; Preston "Teddy" Holden, deputy assessor; Hall Maxwell, county clerk; and Dolores Scott Underwood, deputy. (Courtesy Doddridge County Historical Society.)

This image of the Gain home, which was located on the left fork of Arnold's Creek, was taken May 30, 1905. James P. Gain is shown with an unidentified woman and two of his children. (Courtesy Doddridge County Historical Society.)

Elizabeth Hardesty and Norman McIntyre appear in this photo taken at the Central Station No. 30 pump station. Jo and Art Dotson donated the photo. (Courtesy Doddridge County Historical Society.)

Ward Currey of Doddridge County stands atop an oxen yoke. Among those on the ground below him are John Ford and Albert Currey, also from Doddridge County. The photo was taken in Tucker County, *c.* 1900. (Courtesy Doddridge County Historical Society.)

(Left) In the early 1900s, Ida Jane Warner owned a millinery store that was located next to the Bonnell Apartments in West Union. She later moved her business to the Main Street building that became the First National Bank. (Courtesy Doddridge County Historical Society.)
(Right) This cameo photo shows Nettie Smith Swentzel, who was born on October 15, 1902. She was the wife of Earl Swentzel and the mother of Alvin Swentzel. (Courtesy Doddridge County Historical Society.)

Silas Ellsworth McIntyre walks around his home at Morgan's Run in eastern Doddridge County in 1944. This area is now known as the Double W, and all the old buildings are gone. The woodlands are owned by McIntyre's descendants. (Courtesy Larry G. Williams Sr.)

Mr. and Mrs. Charles Freel Williams, the parents of Larry G. Williams Sr., are among the folks shown here going Christmas tree hunting in 1931 on Leeson's Run, located off Greenwood Hill Road in western Doddridge County. (Courtesy Larry G. Williams Sr.)

This photo provided by Larry G. Williams Sr. shows, from a distance, the old homestead of his father, Charles Freel Williams, located along Leeson's Run. Note the "worm fence" that surrounds the property.

Fred Zinn proudly holds his catch of an 11-pound, 2-ounce muskie while holding a 30.30 rifle in the other. The photo, provided by Larry G. Williams Sr., was taken in a rural section somewhere in Doddridge County.

Two

BUSINESS AND INDUSTRY

The advent of the railroad around 1856 naturally acted as the stimulus to the town of West Union. Toward the end of the century, oil began making its move into Doddridge County as a primary industry and would remain that way for several years. Previously, the county had derived most of its support from the farmers, cattlemen, and timbermen. Quite a number of smaller businesses followed, not only into West Union, but also into other communities such as Smithburg, New Milton, Center Point, Greenwood, and Leopold. Some evidence of this is seen on the following pages.

This scene of a mine tipple and a border house with a worker driving a mule in the foreground was taken from a postcard. It is uncertain who sent the postcard, but the John and Hattie Hafer Estate donated the card. (Courtesy Doddridge County Historical Society.)

West Union, West Va. ______________ 192__

To Midland Electric Service Co **Dr.**

------------ K. W. Reading ------------	
------------ K. W. Reading ------------	
------------ K. W. Consumed ------------	
------------ K. W. at 12 cts. ------------	
------------ K. W. at 6 cts. ------------	
Less 5 % if paid on or before **10th of month**	
Paid by check No. ------------------------	
Minimum charge $1.00 per month.	
No discount after 10th of month.	
Bring this bill with you.	
Received payment	

Collectors Coupon

Discount

Net

The above is an example of a 1926 electric bill from Midland Electric Service Co. of West Union. The amount pales in comparison to today's utility bills. (Courtesy Doddridge County Historical Society.)

This picture postcard shows a large crowd waiting for the train at the West Union Baltimore & Ohio depot. The Ireland Estate donated the postcard. (Courtesy Doddridge County Historical Society.)

The Ideal Window Glass Co. was one of West Union's better-known industries. Note the railroad line and bridge on the left of this photo, donated by Paul and Ruth Cropp. (Courtesy Doddridge County Historical Society.)

This photo, donated by Gregg Smith, provides a view of the Doddridge County Bank, a three-story brick building at the corner of Main and Columbia Streets in West Union. (Courtesy Doddridge County Historical Society.)

The photograph below shows the First National Bank in West Union prior to the 20th century. (Courtesy Doddridge County Historical Society.)

Paul Robinson, wearing the hat, and Lathrop Russell stand in the doorway of the Doddridge County Bank in this early 1900s image, donated by Gregg Smith. (Courtesy Doddridge County Historical Society.)

This building was located on Columbia Street in West Union and housed the Ida Warner Millinery Shop. Betty Langfitt donated the photograph. (Courtesy Doddridge County Historical Society.)

A sawmill located on Arnold's Creek is depicted in the image above, donated by Evelyn Furner Calhoun. The lumber industry has been quite active in Doddridge County through the years. (Courtesy Doddridge County Historical Society.)

Oil and gas drilling was a thriving industry in Doddridge County in the late 19th and early 20th centuries. Bob and Mabel Wagner donated this postcard. (Courtesy Doddridge County Historical Society.)

The lamp black factory at Smithton (now Smithburg) was one of the unique industries of Doddridge County in the 1800s and 1900s. (Courtesy Doddridge County Historical Society.)

The Old Grist Mill on Middle Island Creek appears in this picture postcard. (Courtesy Doddridge County Historical Society.)

Williams Standard Oil Service Station was located in West Union for many years. It was demolished, and a parking lot was built for the West Union Foodland supermarket. (Courtesy Doddridge County Historical Society.)

Dessie Cox took this picture of the Market Store and the wooden footbridge beside it in 1914. The last name of the girl standing on the bridge was Batton, and Charlie Cox is the man on the porch of the store. Velma Hart donated this photograph. (Courtesy Doddridge County Historical Society.)

The Grove Store building, seen here in the foreground, was demolished in 1947 or 1948. On the right is the Grove Hotel, which featured 22 rooms. It was demolished in 1952. Gary Ruppert donated the photo. (Courtesy Doddridge County Historical Society.)

Standard Store Co. of West Union provided shopping bags with its name printed on the side for the convenience of customers who shopped at the store. (Courtesy Doddridge County Historical Society.)

This photo of the second home of the old West Union Bank Building was taken from the late Alton Childers collection. The Flower Connection, a florist business, was located on the ground floor in later years. (Courtesy Doddridge County Historical Society.)

Three

WEST UNION

West Union is located on a 20,000-acre tract of land once owned by James Caldwell. He sold the 20,000 acres to Nathan Davis and his two brothers, William and Joseph, in the early 19th century, and the Davis family moved to what is today West Union. Not long after, the family sold 16,000 acres of the tract to Lewis Maxwell, who was a congressman from Virginia, for the price of 23¢ per acre. Matthew Neeley, grandfather of U.S. Senator and Gov. M. Matthew Neeley, was one of the first pioneers to establish a home in the area, along with Jacob Riley, John Smith, and Joseph Jeffrey. In this chapter photos of numerous familiar landmarks can be seen.

This aerial view shows West Union in 1990. Middle Island Creek runs through the town. Bob and Sara Bailey donated the photo. (Courtesy Doddridge County Historical Society.)

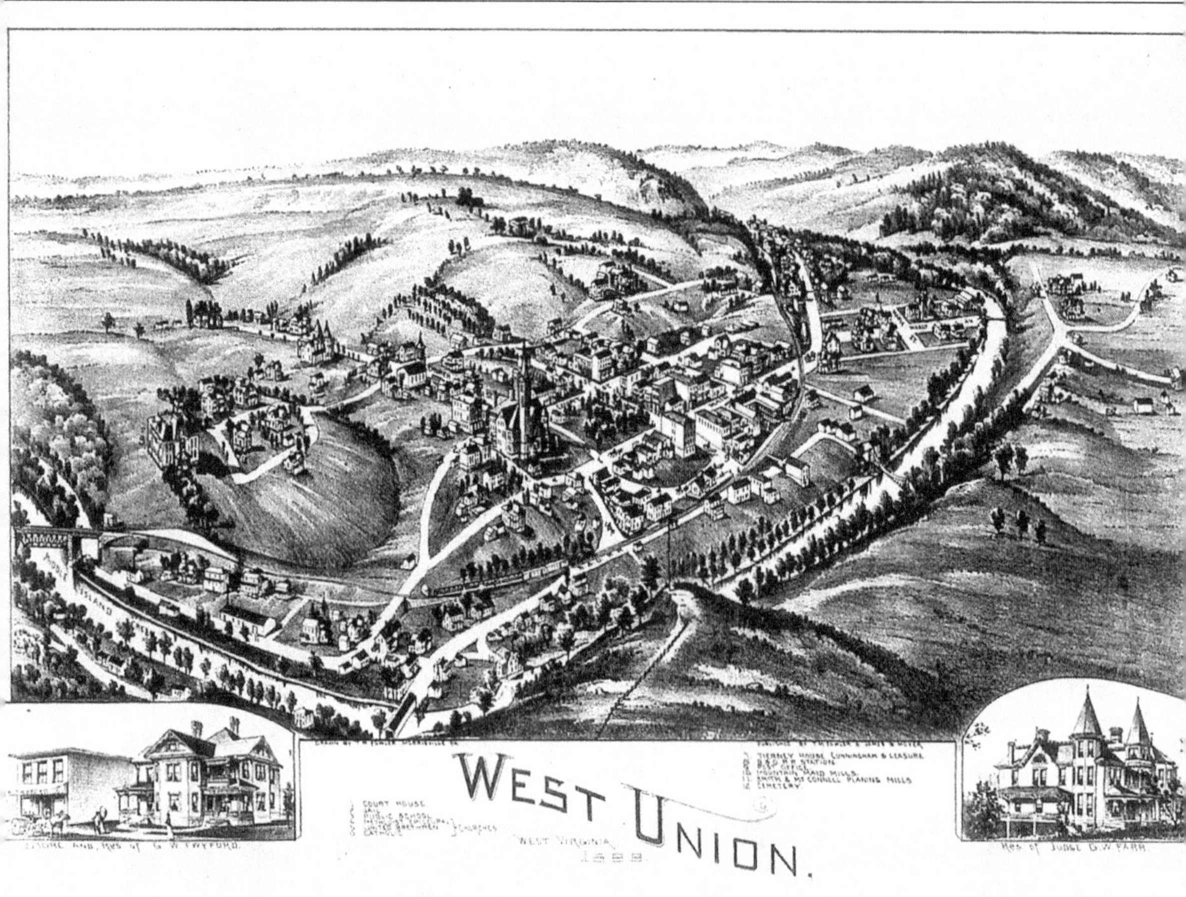

This is artist T.M. Fowler's topographic sketch of the town of West Union, c. 1899. Fowler and James Moyer published the sketch. (Courtesy Doddridge County Historical Society.)

Merchants were generally busy in the central business district of West Union in the early 1900s. The sign for Star Furniture Co. is partially hidden in the lower left of this photo. (Courtesy Doddridge County Historical Society.)

This photo shows an early 20th-century view of Neeley Avenue in West Union. (Courtesy Doddridge County Historical Society.)

Harry N. Twyford of West Union, a commercial artist, stands beside a promotional poster he had just completed. The contents of the poster show the prominence of Twyford and his work. (Courtesy Doddridge County Historical Society.)

Pictured here in August 1974 is the Doddridge County Courthouse in West Union with its familiar clock tower. (Courtesy Doddridge County Historical Society.)

The steps and front entrance to the Doddridge County Courthouse in West Union, the seat of government in the county, are visible in this 1957 photo, donated by Jo and Art Dotson. (Courtesy Doddridge County Historical Society.)

This road crew poses while they work on West Virginia Route 18 North in front of the West Union Grade School. The sign reads, "W.Va. Relief Administration Works Division." Bob and Mabel Wagner donated the photo. (Courtesy Doddridge County Historical Society.)

This 1957 photograph shows Church Street and the sidewalk in front of private residences and a church. Jo and Art Dotson donated the image. (Courtesy Doddridge County Historical Society.)

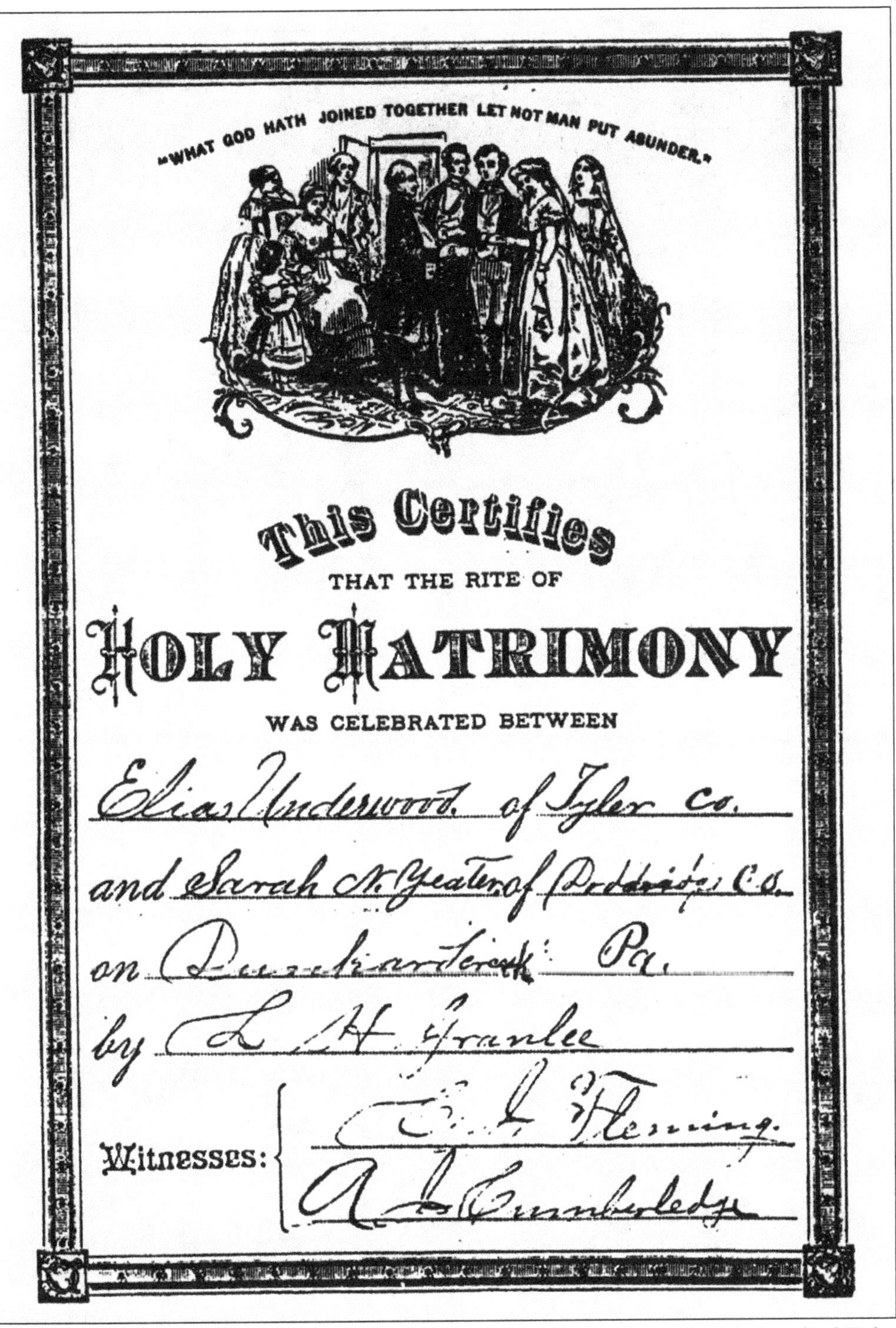

"WHAT GOD HATH JOINED TOGETHER LET NOT MAN PUT ASUNDER."

This Certifies

THAT THE RITE OF

HOLY MATRIMONY

WAS CELEBRATED BETWEEN

Elias Underwood of Tyler Co.

and Sarah N. Yeater of Doddridge Co.

on [illegible] Pa.

by L. H. Granlee

Witnesses: [illegible] Fleming

[illegible] Cumberledge

This document shows an old, undated certificate of marriage for Elias Underwood of Tyler County and Sarah N. Yeater of Doddridge County. They were married by L.H. Granlee, and individuals named only as Fleming and Cumberledge witnessed the union. (Courtesy Doddridge County Historical Society.)

The James Foley home on East Main Street in West Union is shown here. Mr. Foley is shown at the far left, and Townsend Davis is second from the right. The other two men are unidentified in this photo donated by Glade Willis. (Courtesy Doddridge County Historical Society.)

The Ray C. Smith house at 405 West Main Street in West Union appears in this photo donated by the Oma Corder Estate. (Courtesy Doddridge County Historical Society.)

A prominent West Union lawyer, Scott Stuart built this elaborate, twin-towered, Victorian-style home some time in the 19th century. The house still stands today. Toward the latter part of his life, Stuart ordered that a swimming pool be installed, but he died before it could be completed. Mrs. Stella May bought the house and is the current owner.

This brick building is where attorney Scott Stuart had his law office. It is located between the home he built (top photo) and the Doddridge County Historical Society Museum. It is today used for storage and contains Stuart's law books. It was probably built before Stuart's house was constructed. Stuart later shared his law practice with Clyde Ware.

On September 5, 1951, a group of interested citizens of Doddridge County appeared before the county commission to request that they establish and maintain a public library. This is the Doddridge County public library's buff-colored, two-story brick building, located across the street from the courthouse, where the library continues to operate to this day. The building formerly housed the Opera House.

This photo, from the Alton Childers collection, shows the Charlie Fleming house, an older home in the Sunnyside area located west of West Union. (Courtesy Doddridge County Historical Society.)

The three-story, brick building that housed the old Masonic Hall in West Union was photographed in later years. The Alton Childers collection donated the photo. (Courtesy Doddridge County Historical Society.)

A prize buck hangs upside down near the front porch of what was believed to be the Hardesty residence in this photo donated by Jo and Art Dotson. (Courtesy Doddridge County Historical Society.)

Several shops are visible in this photo donated by Jo and Art Dotson. A parade proceeds through the central business district of West Union, and judging by the parked cars, it seems to have taken place in the late 1940s or early 1950s. (Courtesy Doddridge County Historical Society.)

Here is a view of one of the cells at the old jail, which was located on the second floor of what is now the Doddridge County Historical Society Museum.

These trucks are parked in front of the garage of the Bridge Chevrolet, Inc. dealership in West Union. (Courtesy Doddridge County Historical Society.)

This smokehouse/washing house belonging to Doddridge County native Joseph H. Diss DeBar, the designer of the state seal of West Virginia, was still standing in its original position in the mid-1970s. The property on which the building stood was later owned by Joe Hinter. (Courtesy Doddridge County Historical Society.)

An old, wicker baby buggy appears in this photo donated by Jo and Art Dotson. (Courtesy Doddridge County Historical Society.)

The Blair House is shown in this 1909 image from a picture postcard donated by the Ireland Estate. Standing, from left to right, are Jackson Van Buren Blair, his son Marion Blair, and Jackson's grandsons Monroe Ireland and L. Blair Ireland. (Courtesy Doddridge County Historical Society.)

This photograph depicts the old mill after the devastating 1915 flood. Jacqueline Wetzel donated the image. (Courtesy Doddridge County Historical Society.)

Here is a view of the Charter House in West Union. Billy Kiger donated this photo. (Courtesy Doddridge County Historical Society.)

This three-story brick building in West Union is the Grant House, which once accommodated a number of tenants. (Courtesy Doddridge County Historical Society.)

These sunflowers were photographed somewhere in Doddridge County quite a few years ago. Jo and Art Dotson donated the photo. (Courtesy Doddridge County Historical Society.) .

These three men are surveying an ice gorge near West Union during one of Doddridge County's severe winters of the past. Neva Ritter donated the picture. (Courtesy Doddridge County Historical Society.)

Four

OTHER COMMUNITIES

Although West Union is the largest town in Doddridge County as well as its seat of government, communities such as Greenwood, Big Flint, Sedalia, Oxford, Blandville, Center Point, Smithburg, Big Isaac, Leopold, Central Station, New Milton, and Long Run help make it a county with a great deal of pride. Images representing all of these areas were not available, but every Doddridge Countian is entitled to share the pride of which we speak. One of the county's most recent accomplishments has been to land a site for the regional jail, which will be just off Route 50 on Wilhelm Run Road and provide a number of jobs.

"Dad" Hitchcock and his son Paul ran the Pure Oil Gas Station at Greenwood in western Doddridge County. This photo was donated by Delbert Wilson. (Courtesy Doddridge County Historical Society.)

Dwayne Ellifritt, another talented Doddridge Countian, painted this picture of Victor Ellifritt's general store located in the Greenwood area. (Courtesy Doddridge County Historical Society.)

The Long Run Store, seen here in an image donated by Billy Kiger, is located in extreme eastern Doddridge County. The store remains standing today. (Courtesy Doddridge County Historical Society.)

The Racket Store at New Milton in southern Doddridge County appears in this c. 1907 photo. As the sign says, the business sold hats, shoes, clothing, and other dry goods. (Courtesy Doddridge County Historical Society.)

Donated by Anne Devine Hurst, this picture shows Lloyd Mowrey's store at Big Isaac. The store later became a casualty of the May 7, 1918 flood. The house on the distant left was the residence of Leonard Slussar, and the one in the center is D.W. "Dallas" Bell's residence and studio. (Courtesy Doddridge County Historical Society.)

These are the remains of the Glen Bennett house following the May 1918 flooding at Big Isaac in eastern Doddridge County. (Courtesy Doddridge County Historical Society.)

Bill and Mary Calhoun donated both of these postcards depicting the Leopold community. Above, cars inch down a Leopold street. Below, a quiet street scene is void of people or cars. (Courtesy Doddridge County Historical Society.)

This photo shows the heavy damage in the basement of a drug store in Doddridge County that resulted from a major fire that occurred some time in the mid-20th century. The photo was from Alton Childers's collection. (Courtesy Doddridge County Historical Society.)

This *c.* 1959 photo, donated by Jo and Art Dotson, shows old U.S. Route 50 at the Smithburg cut. The four-lane U.S. 50 replaced this segment of road in the 1970s. (Courtesy Doddridge County Historical Society.)

The fire at the K&W Tourist Home, on the corner of old Route 50 and Neeley Avenue in West Union, was one of the most devastating in Doddridge County's history. Bob and Mabel Wagner donated the photo in memory of Roy and Vonda Wagner. (Courtesy Doddridge County Historical Society.)

A replica of an old-fashioned "operating room" was created on the ground floor of the Doddridge County Historical Society Museum.

The store known as the Little Ritz, pictured above, was owned and operated by Mr. and Mrs. W.D. Wilfong. The store was located along old Route 50 a mile west of Greenwood near the Doddridge-Ritchie county line. (Courtesy Doddridge County Historical Society.)

These five, similarly dressed, but unidentified ladies are standing on a wooden footbridge outside the Ore Coffman home along West Virginia Route 23 near Center Point. Anne Mish provided this c. 1910 photo.

REGISTRY RETURN RECEIPT sent Jan 25, 1895

Reg. No. 4 from Post Office at SMITHTON, - W. VA.

*Reg. Letter
~~Reg. Parcel~~ Addressed to F A Lang
Clarksburg W Va

After obtaining receipt below, the Postmaster will mail this Card, without cover and without postage, to address on the other side.

RECEIVED THE ABOVE DESCRIBED REGISTERED *LETTER. ~~PARCEL.~~

(SENDER'S NAME ON OTHER SIDE.)

Sign on dotted lines to the right.

When delivery is made to other than addressee, the name of both addressee and recipient must appear.

Fred A Lang

Albert Lang

* Erase letter or parcel according to which is sent.

Above is a postal registry return receipt dated January 25, 1895 and addressed to F.A. Lang of Clarksburg. It was postmarked at Smithton, now Smithburg. (Courtesy Larry G. Williams Sr.)

H.B. Williams built his family's home at Cabin Run in western Doddridge County in 1880. The house was reroofed in 1999. (Courtesy Larry G. Williams Sr.)

Part II

RITCHIE COUNTY

Ritchie County, formed in 1843 from parts of Harrison, Lewis, and Wood Counties, was named for Thomas Ritchie, a distinguished journalist from Richmond, Virginia, whose mother was the sister of Judge Spencer Roane, for whom Roane County was named. The county's size is 455.27 square miles and its county seat is Harrisville. It is bounded on the north by Pleasants and Tyler Counties; on the east by Doddridge; on the south by Gilmer, Calhoun, and Wirt; and on the west by Wirt and Wood.

At the first census following its creation, Ritchie County's population was 3,856, but by 1910, it had increased to near 20,000.

Five

Railroads and More

The Baltimore & Ohio Railroad line that stretched east and west across Ritchie County eventually became the focal point for the transportation of people and freight. Other railroads included the Ritchie Mines, Calico Railroad, and Cairo and Kanawha Valley (C&K) Railroad. Also, countless oil wells could be found in Ritchie County, especially in Cornwallis, Cairo, and Auburn. Other lucrative trades like lumbering and agriculture were by no means lacking, as witnessed on the next several pages.

This old locomotive, hauling a number of freight cars, pulled out of the Cairo train station some time in the late 19th century. (Courtesy Ritchie County Historical Society.)

This standard gauge locomotive sat on a trestle of the Harrisville Southern Railroad at Cornwallis in the early 19th century. (Courtesy Ritchie County Historical Society.)

The original owner of this photo claimed it showed a C&K engine, but some experts in railroads of the 19th century disagree. Note that logs were used for railroad ties. (Courtesy Ritchie County Historical Society.)

The Silver Run No. 19 tunnel is one of numerous railroad tunnels that were used for years in Ritchie County. At a length of 1,376 feet, the tunnel is all brick and, as some bicyclists have attested, rather damp inside. (Courtesy Diana Druga.)

The B&O Railroad depot at Pennsboro in eastern Ritchie County, pictured here in the 1940s, stood in front of the Wells Building. (Courtesy Ritchie County Historical Society.)

The B&O depot at Ellenboro, on the right, is unique in appearance because unlike most other railroad stations, the "Ellenboro" sign is parallel with the line rather than facing the approaching trains. (Courtesy Ritchie County Historical Society.)

These railroad lines pass through Pennsboro. In this bird's-eye view looking west, the Pennsboro depot of the B&O is just to the right of the United Woodworking Co. (Courtesy Ritchie County Historical Society.)

The Laurel Fork and Sand Hill Railroad engine "Sterling" (standard gauge) is seen above. The railroad extended from the B&O line to Volcano in Wood County. (Courtesy Ritchie County Historical Society.)

A number of railroad officials and spectators crowd around a major train wreck on the C&K Railroad at Cairo in the early 20th century. Numerous train wrecks took place in Ritchie County. (Courtesy Ritchie County Historical Society.)

This streetcar pulls into the town of Lamberton, near Ellenboro, on Independence Day, 1919. (Courtesy Ritchie County Historical Society.)

Above, the well-known *St. Louis Express* passes through Cairo over this trestle around the early 1900s. Note the women in the right foreground at the end of the footbridge. (Courtesy Ritchie County Historical Socicty.)

Grant Luzader photographed this multi-car train derailment at Toll Gate in eastern Ritchie County. (Courtesy Ritchie County Historical Society.)

The Harvey and N.D. Marsh Store is shown in this 1899 picture taken in Cornwallis. The town became an active B&O station when the timber industry was "king." Also, note the oil derrick on the left. (Courtesy Ritchie County Historical Society.)

L. Schoolcraft photographed this *c.* 1913 bird's-eye view of Cairo. Both the oil and gas and railroad industries are represented in the view. The track and depot of the C&K Railroad are on the right. (Courtesy Ritchie County Historical Society.)

The No. 20 tunnel is shown here being removed in 1963. The crew and equipment are facing the tunnel. (Courtesy Alan Nichols for Ritchie County Historical Society.)

In the background of this photo is the railroad depot at Petroleum. (Courtesy Ritchie County Historical Society.)

These railroad workers stand atop the C&K Railroad and at the Macfarland depot in the southern part of the county. (Courtesy Ritchie County Historical Society.)

Milton Isner and friends take a break from work while constructing a well house at one of the many oil and gas operations in the county. (Courtesy Ritchie County Historical Society.)

Shown in this photograph is the oldest oil well rig and oilfield in Ritchie County; it is located near Cairo. (Courtesy Ritchie County Historical Society.)

Located east of Cairo, the No. 18 tunnel, pictured here, was removed in the early 1960s. The Confederate Rebels had burned it out during the War between the States. (Courtesy Ritchie County Historical Society.)

W.H. Mossor stands beside his vehicle at a cane mill at Thursday, a community located along West Virginia Route 47 between Smithville and Burnt House. (Courtesy Ritchie County Historical Society.)

This photo shows the Premium Glass Co. at Pennsboro in the mid-20th century. (Courtesy Ritchie County Historical Society.)

The B&O Railroad depot at Pennsboro appears in this early 1900s photo with (from left) Lacy's Millinery, Fleming's Bakery, the McGinnis Hotel, and the Wells Building. (Courtesy Ritchie County Historical Society.)

Two well workers take a break from building a wooden tank at an oilfield in 20th-century Ritchie County. (Courtesy Ritchie County Historical Society.)

This group of men, young and old, relaxes outside the Bill Dotson store along the C&K Railroad track at Mellin in western Ritchie County. (Courtesy Vivian Dotson for Ritchie County Historical Society.)

The natural gas pump station at Cornwallis in the western half of the county appears above. (Courtesy J. Paugh for Ritchie County Historical Society.)

This old converted railroad car served as the Harrisville Southern Combine at Harrisville. (Courtesy Ritchie County Historical Society.)

The Harrisville Southern Railroad Depot, located at Harrisville, is pictured here in the 1930s. (Courtesy Steve Davidson for Ritchie County Historical Society.)

Six

HARRISVILLE, PENNSBORO, AND CAIRO

Ritchie County's seat, Harrisville, and the towns of Pennsboro and Cairo are the largest communities in the county. Although continued growth was slow in Harrisville during the first half of the 20th century, the community has witnessed much development since the early 1960s, especially in the garment industry. In contrast, Pennsboro prospered from the beginning of the 19th century to the mid-20th century with the arrival of a glass factory and other industries that followed, as well as numerous retail stores. Then there is Cairo, the community that is seven years older than the State of West Virginia and was initially called Egypt by the early settlers due to its fertile farmland. This chapter features many images that recall the past for Ritchie Countians.

Shown in this photo is a pipeyard behind the South Side Service Station at Harrisville. (Courtesy Steve Davidson for Ritchie County Historical Society.)

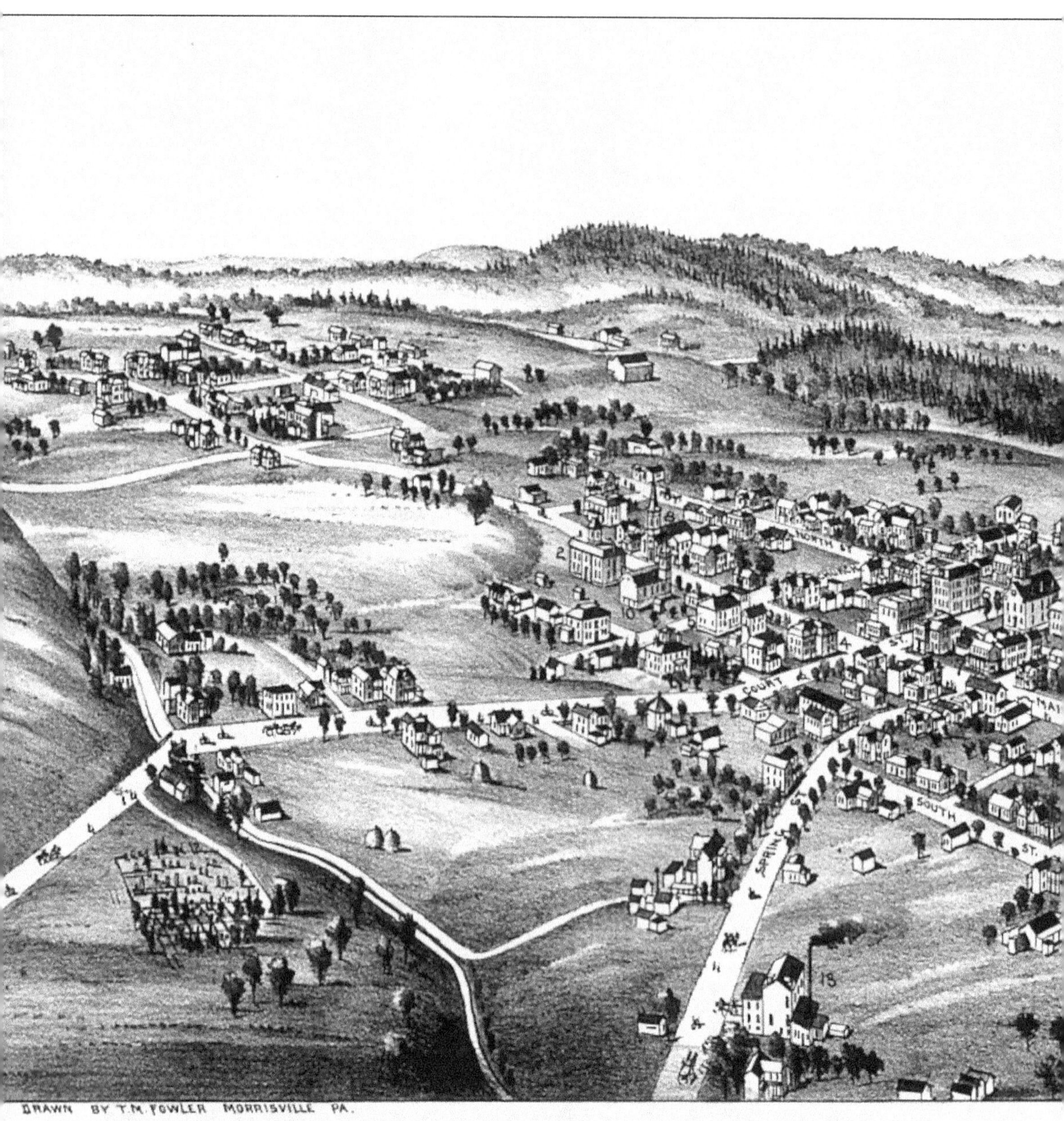

DRAWN BY T.M. FOWLER MORRISVILLE PA.

1. COURT HOUSE.
2. PUBLIC SCHOOL.
3. P.&H. R.R. STATION.
4. POST OFFICE.
5. OPERA HOUSE.
6. WHITE HALL HOTEL B.F. PATTON
7. WATSON HOUSE.

HARRISV

RITCHIE COUNTY W

1899.

This is a sketch of the city of Harrisville dated 1899. T.M. Fowler and James B. Moyer originally published the sketch, while T.M. Fowler of Morrisville, Pennsylvania drew it. (Courtesy David M. Scott)

On May 30, 1923, these servicemen were on hand in Harrisville for the laying of the cornerstone of the new Ritchie County Courthouse. (Courtesy Steve Davidson for Ritchie County Historical Society)

This c. 1930 picture shows the Ritchie County Courthouse in Harrisville dominated by its familiar clock tower. (Courtesy Ritchie County Historical Society.)

A bicyclist pedals down Main Street in the business district of Harrisville in the late 1920s or early 1930s. The Broadwater Building is the last building visible in the background. (Courtesy Ritchie County Historical Society.)

The People's Bank, shown above when it was located on Court Street, later became the site of the Union Bank. (Courtesy Ritchie County Historical Society.)

Taken in about 1915, this image shows the First National Bank in Harrisville, founded in 1906. The federal post office was located on the ground level at the far left end of the building. (Courtesy David M. Scott.)

This uniformed group of men, the Modern Woodsmen, hold a drill on the lawn of the Ritchie County Courthouse in Harrisville. (Courtesy Ritchie County Historical Society.)

Photographed in the mid-1950s, the Morris Building was one of the landmarks in the business district of Harrisville. At left is the Great Atlantic & Pacific Tea Co., better known as the A&P. (Courtesy Ritchie County Historical Society.)

Located at the corner of South Spring and Pierpoint Streets was Snyder Brothers Garage. Note the old-fashioned gasoline pump at far right. (Courtesy Ritchie County Historical Society.)

Harrisville High School was situated atop this hill more than 75 years ago. In the late 20th century, however, Harrisville High consolidated with the other high schools in the county to form the new Ritchie County High School, which is located just off four-lane U.S. Route 50 at Ellenboro. (Courtesy Ritchie County Historical Society.)

This *c.* 1910 photo shows a group of people, including administrators, teachers, and students, from the Summer Normal School at Harrisville. (Courtesy Ritchie County Historical Society.)

The gas street lamp at left in this Main Street view, looking west, was typical of late 19th-century Harrisville. The business at left is Martin's Harness & Stables. (Courtesy Ritchie County Historical Society.)

This c. 1955 image also features Main Street looking west, although a number of years later. A women's clothing store and the corner Rexall Drug store are visible. (Courtesy Ritchie County Historical Society.)

Around 1897, a spectacular fire destroyed the Stout Hardware Store located on South Spring Street. (Courtesy Ritchie County Historical Society.)

The Harrisville High School baseball team owned the proud distinction of being the state champions in 1963. (Courtesy Ritchie County Historical Society.)

Hezekiah Boyers Williams stands in front of the cellar of his house on Cabin Run east of Pennsboro in Ritchie County. He was a veteran of the War between the States and the great grandfather of Larry G. Williams Sr., who provided the photo.

This sketch by T.M. Fowler shows a glimpse of the town of Pennsboro in 1899. Fowler and James B. Moyer originally published the sketch. (Courtesy Ritchie County Historical Society.)

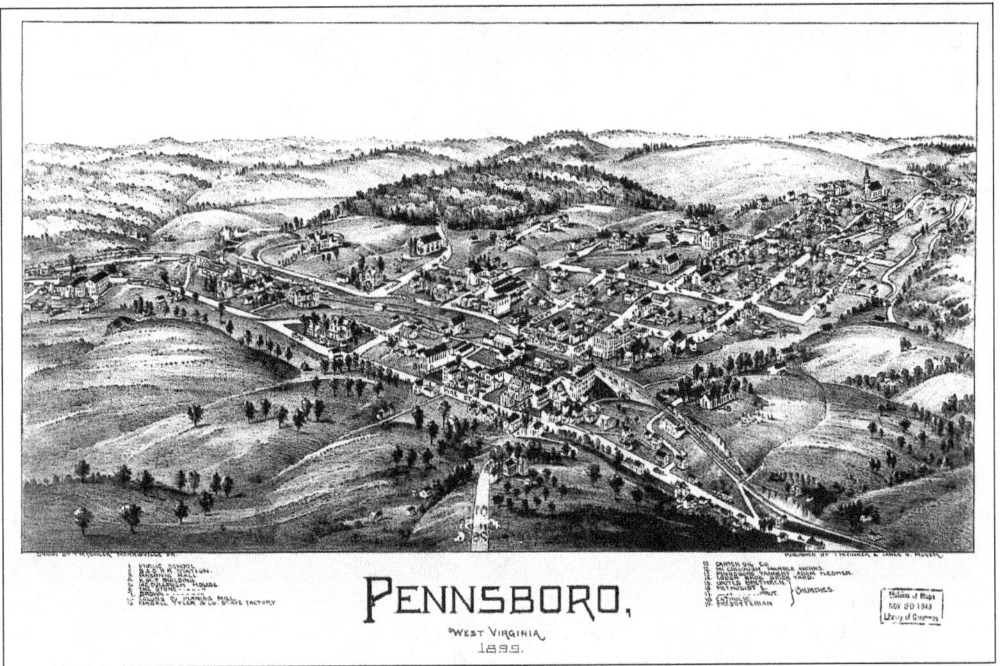

Cecil Ridgeway's Gulf service station was located at Pennsboro along old Route 50 in the mid-1950s. (Courtesy Larry G. Williams Sr.)

This small bear, halfway up a utility pole in front of the T. Lambert store and Citizens National Bank in Pennsboro, must have been looking for a "honey" of a deal. Dr. A.P. Jones's office was located on the second floor of the bank building. (Courtesy Ritchie County Historical Society.)

The former Pennsboro High School sat atop this knoll in Pennsboro. It consolidated with Harrisville, Cairo, and other high schools in the 1980s to become Ritchie County High School at Ellenboro. (Courtesy Ritchie County Historical Society.)

Jim Williamson, third from the left in this *c.* 1911 image, was the owner of Dry Goods & Groceries (the building on the far right) in Pennsboro. Williamson's wife operated a Pennsboro millinery. The Wells Building later occupied this site. (Courtesy Ritchie County Historical Society.)

Members of the Pennsboro High School track team of 1921 appear here. They became state champions that year under the leadership of Coach H.K. Rowley (back row, left). (Courtesy Ritchie County Historical Society.)

This may well have been the scene of an Independence Day parade along South Main Street in Pennsboro. In the background can be seen the M.K. Duty home, later used as the Pennsboro American Legion home. (Courtesy Ritchie County Historical Society.)

The Rose Marie Tearoom in the Arlington Hotel in Pennsboro was the apparent destination of the lady in the right foreground. A Mrs. Grimm managed the tearoom. Wooden steps can be seen leading up to Church Street. (Courtesy Ritchie County Historical Society.)

With the B&O Railroad line visible in the foreground, this view shows the east end of Pennsboro. (Courtesy Ritchie County Historical Society.)

The Pennsboro Public School, built in 1890, had 235 pupils by 1910. (Courtesy Ritchie County Historical Society.)

Bert Bradford, in the straw hat, managed the Pennsboro baseball team in 1908. (Courtesy Ritchie County Historical Society.)

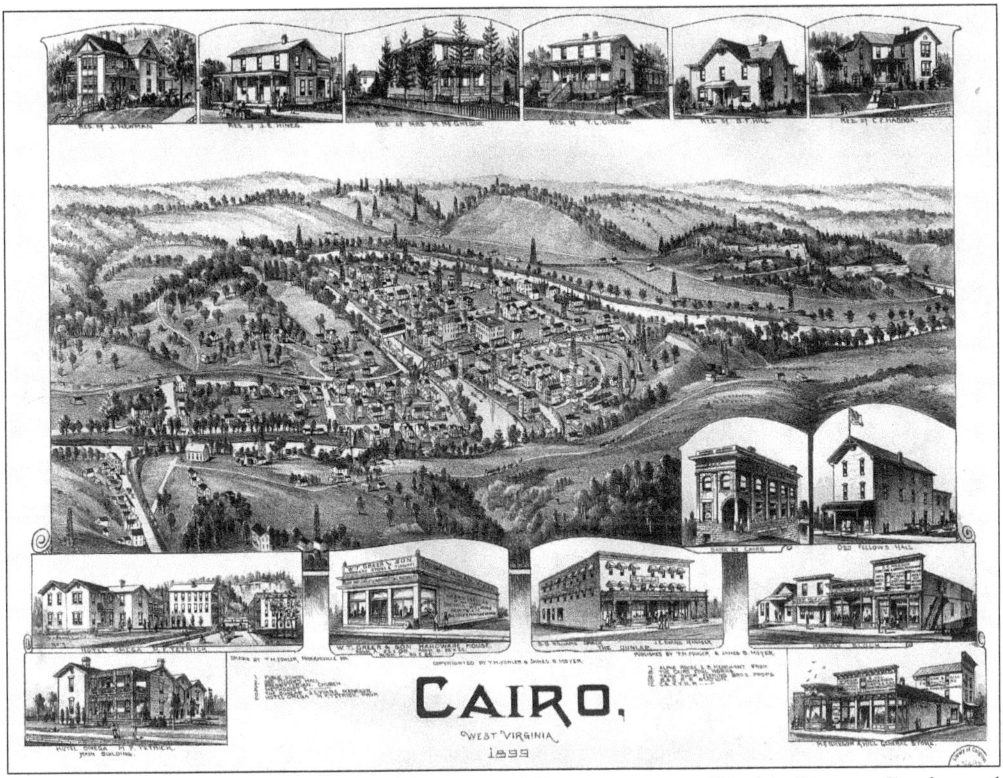

CAIRO,
WEST VIRGINIA
1899

T.M. Fowler completed this sketch of the town of Cairo in western Ritchie County. Fowler and James B. Moyer published the sketch. (Courtesy Ritchie County Historical Society.)

(Left) This is the Bank of Cairo in the 1920s. It was named to the National Register of Historic Places in later years. (Courtesy Ritchie County Historical Society.)
(Right) This Fourth of July celebration is seen from the top of the bank building. (Courtesy Ritchie County Historical Society.)

This is Cairo High School, *c.* 1940. It would be consolidated with the county's other high schools in the 1980s to become Ritchie County High School. (Courtesy Ritchie County Historical Society.)

Oral J. Heckler, in white, directed the Cairo High School Band in the 1950s. (Courtesy Ritchie County Historical Society.)

Cairo's opera house was housed on the second floor of this building in 1910, and McGregor & Co.'s warehouse was on the ground floor. (Courtesy Ritchie County Historical Society.)

This photograph shows Luther Ramsey, N.D. Marsh, and Lyle Goff standing in front of the Ramsey, Silcott & Co. store. The date of the photograph is unknown. (Courtesy Ritchie County Historical Society.)

This is McGregor Avenue in Cairo, c. 1914. The building at right housed the Raiguel Funeral Home. (Courtesy Ritchie County Historical Society.)

When Cairo held its centennial celebration in May 1956, this horse-drawn hearse was Raiguel Funeral Home's parade entry. (Courtesy Ritchie County Historical Society.)

Would you or perhaps your relatives recognize any of the individuals who were part of the 1908 class of the Cairo Normal School, shown here? (Courtesy Ritchie County Historical Society.)

Cairo High School fielded a baseball team in 1953. Are there any of these team members, or the coach, who may be known to you? (Courtesy Ritchie County Historical Society.)

These associates at Cairo Mercantile Co., shown in 1916, are from left to right, George Caton, N.D. Marsh, Charles Myers, Luther Ramsey, and Roscoe Moats. (Courtesy Ritchie County Historical Society.)

This is the swinging bridge that spanned the Hughes River to the west end of Cairo. The photo was taken in the late 19th or early 20th century. (Courtesy Ritchie County Historical Society.)

Seven

Other Communities

Pullman, Ellenboro, Smithville, and Macfarlan are just some of the small communities in Ritchie County. The folks who live in and around them hopefully will especially enjoy looking back in time at how things once looked in their neighborhoods. Cornwallis, Auburn, Berea, and Tollgate are a few of the neighborhoods that help form Ritchie County. Ritchie County is also home to North Bend State Park, a beautiful and popular recreational facility in the hills of the western portion of the county. Not every town and village could be represented in the images collected for this chapter, but here are some that will likely spark many a conversation.

Earl Drey, the owner of Drey's Restaurant at Ellenboro, is shown here with Edith Barnes. The window sign reads, "Quick Lunch - Ice Cream & Sodas. Ladies & Gents Dining Room." (Courtesy Ritchie County Historical Society.)

This is a bird's-eye view of the town of Ellenboro, photographed in 1916. (Courtesy Ritchie County Historical Society.)

The two-lane highway shown here is West Virginia Route 16 at Ellenboro. The photo was taken in September 1993. (Courtesy Larry G. Williams Sr.)

The student body of Ellenboro Grade School appears as in front of their building in the early 20th century. (Courtesy Ritchie County Historical Society.)

Looking west, this bird's-eye view shows the town of Pullman in the eastern portion of Ritchie County. (Courtesy Ritchie County Historical Society.)

Pullman State Bank was established in the community in 1902. It closed in 1930 just after the start of the Great Depression, as many banks did. The individuals in front of the establishment are not identified. (Courtesy Ritchie County Historical Society.)

The community of Tollgate appears in this early 20th-century photo. Zinn Planing Mill was located behind the white cottage. (Courtesy Ritchie County Historical Society.)

Here is the Broadwater Feed Store at Tollgate, which burned in 1905 but was rebuilt at a nearby site. Tollgate is near the Ritchie-Doddridge county line. (Courtesy Ritchie County Historical Society.)

Washington Inn stands above a swimming pool along old U.S. Route 50 in the community of Lamberton, near Ellenboro. (Courtesy Ritchie County Historical Society.)

In 1817, the first post office in this community was called Federal Hill and it lasted four years. In 1938, Mole Hill was established. It's name was changed to "Mountain" 111 years later, a unique example of making a Mountain out of a Mole Hill. (Courtesy Ritchie County Historical Society.)

This is a c. 1908 bird's-eye view of the community of Berea, which was first settled in 1848 and photographed nearly a century ago. (Courtesy Ritchie County Historical Society.)

This historic marker at the Ritchie County line gives a "thumbnail" history of the county. Larry G. Williams Sr. of Munroe Falls, Ohio, photographed the marker, which stands near the old Carnegie Gas station near Pennsboro. (Courtesy Larry G. Williams Sr.)

Named for Barnes Smith, the town of Smithville, in the extreme southern part of the county, was chartered in 1842. Here, the town is shown in the devastating 1950 flood. (Courtesy Ritchie County Historical Society.)

Built in 1875, the Smithville Methodist Episcopal Church, above, was struck by lightning in 1922 and burned to the ground. (Courtesy Ritchie County Historical Society.)

Two unidentified men stand on the Staunton Pike Bridge at Macfarlan in the late 1800s. Macfarlan is located on West Virginia Route 47 in the southern part of the county. (Courtesy Ritchie County Historical Society.)

These six gentlemen are not identified, but the structure shown behind them is the Morgan House, where many a traveler along the Staunton Pike (later Route 47) would stay overnight. (Courtesy Ritchie County Historical Society.)

These brave souls stand nearly midway across the wooden swinging bridge that spans Otterslide near the community of Berea. It is doubtful that many today would venture onto such a precariously situated bridge. (Courtesy Ritchie County Historical Society.)

In 1910, the "beehive" of the small Ritchie County community of Washburn was the Hall & Brothers store. (Courtesy Ritchie County Historical Society.)

The little girl (front row, third from right) holds a small slate on which is written, "First Grade of Mellin School, Oct. 31, '13." The tiny community of Mellin is located near Macfarlan. (Courtesy Ritchie County Historical Society.)

One of the most popular events to take place each year was the Ritchie County Fair. The fairgrounds were located at Pennsboro in the eastern part of the county; however, the fair is no more. All the buildings have been demolished. The race track remained, but for racecars, not race horses. There are many fond memories of the fair. (Courtesy Ritchie County Historical Society.)

The Petroleum Presbyterian Church, seen here in the early 20th century, was surrounded by a white picket fence. It later became a Methodist church. (Courtesy Ritchie County Historical Society.)

This wood frame structure housed the Perrine Store in the Ritchie County town of Petroleum. One of the railroad lines that went through the county passed directly in front of this store. (Courtesy Ritchie County Historical Society.)

The building at right is the Mount Olivet Methodist Episcopal Church, which was dedicated in 1886, at Finch. Whiskey Run School can be seen on the hill, just to the left of the church. (Courtesy Ritchie County Historical Society.)

H.A. "Barney" Hardman stands behind the tire tube in front of the Hardman Garage/Auburn Motor Company, which was a Chevrolet dealer and sold Sinclair HC Gasoline. A movie theater was housed upstairs. (Courtesy Ritchie County Historical Society.)

This log structure, photographed by Ritchie County historian Grant Luzader, was just one of a number of mills located in the county. The exact location of it was not disclosed. (Courtesy Ritchie County Historical Society.)

A bell hung over the far end of Cairo's swinging bridge, just to the left of the bank building, c. 1916. A railroad/pedestrian bridge subsequently replaced the swinging bridge and railroad bridge. (Courtesy Ritchie County Historical Society.)

A view of Berea prior to the time an addition was put onto the school provided this pastoral scene. (Courtesy Ritchie County Historical Society.)

On June 25, 1950, a disastrous flood hit Ritchie County communities such as Cairo. This is Cairo's Main Street, looking east. (Courtesy Ritchie County Historical Society.)

Eight

Ritchie County Heritage

As with Doddridge and just about any county in West Virginia, the most precious resource of Ritchie County is its people and its rich heritage. Many of the buildings and landmarks seen photographed on preceding pages are still standing, while others have since been demolished. But the memories of Ritchie Countians who have passed on will continue forever. The remaining pages of this book will recall just some of those individuals.

Harold Zinn is behind the wheel of this nifty 1933 Ford Roadster convertible. At left is Ern Zinn, uncle of Pennsboro native Larry G. Williams Sr., who provided this photo, and at right is Larry's father, Fred Williams.

These stockholders of the Mid-Atlantic Glass Co. in Lamberton were likely members of prominent families in Ritchie County. From left to right are the following: (seated) Arvin Wilson, Fred Fraley, L. Casto, Harry McLaughlin, and Lloyd Games; (standing) Joe Rosa, Sestel Valentine, Wilson Casto, Revvie Riggleman, and Otto Serra. (Courtesy Ritchie County Historical Society.)

Mrs. Duane Moats adjusts a hair dryer on the head of customer Mrs. Fred Fraley at the Harrisville Vanity Beauty Shop, which was located above the pharmacy at East Main and South Court Streets. (Courtesy Ritchie County Historical Society.)

This is the Pullman High School graduating class of 1921. Unfortunately, no identification of the members of the class was available, but some may still reside in Ritchie County or have descendants remaining in the area. (Courtesy Ritchie County Historical Society.)

Otto and Stella Chaffee pose for a photo in front of their Ritchie County residence in the early 1900s. (Courtesy Larry G. Williams Sr.)

Andy Hatfield (center of this group and holding a small bell) was the teacher of the students at Hazelgreen School, on what is county Route 19, in 1895. (Courtesy Ritchie County Historical Society.)

This unidentified young chap looks quite busy feeding the chickens outside his home. Note the sloped cellar door at right. (Courtesy Ritchie County Historical Society.)

Bert Moats stands in a doorway at the Cairo Milling Company. He sold flour, corn meal, feed, and hay. (Courtesy Ritchie County Historical Society.)

Peter Thomas, the elderly gentleman wearing the black cap on the left, was one of the Thomas brothers, whose first store was in this building in Pennsboro. The girl in front of him is Ernestine Fester. (Courtesy Ritchie County Historical Society.)

E.A. Luzader, far left, was the teacher of this group of students at the public school in Cornwallis. (Courtesy Ritchie County Historical Society.)

Harley Snodgrass taught students at the Lick Run School in the early part of the 20th century. (Courtesy Ritchie County Historical Society.)

L.C. Goff was the name on the windows of the Juna Store and Post Office on Dry Fork of Spruce Creek. Those individuals on the porch may be familiar to some past and present Ritchie Countians. (Courtesy Ritchie County Historical Society.)

Bob McKeen (seated, center) is shown with his parents (seated, left) and his brothers. All the men in the family were railroaders in Ritchie County. This photo was the property of John Davisson. (Courtesy Ritchie County Historical Society.)

Photographed by Grant Luzader, this bearded gentleman was a farmer in the early to mid-1900s in Ritchie County. He appears to have stacked equipment on top of a row of wooden stumps. (Courtesy Ritchie County Historical Society.)

J.E. Cain was the proprietor of a general store at Nutter Farm on old Route 50 in the early part of the 20th century. Note the old stove visible on the left of the picture. (Courtesy Ritchie County Historical Society.)